The
Hollow Bone
of Healing

Miracles and Messages from
the Quantum Field of Source Energy

PHOENIX RISING STAR

Book Interior and E-book Design by Amit Dey | amitdey2528@gmail.com

Foreward

"The body is a self-healing organism, so it's really about clearing things out of the way so the body can heal itself."

~Barbara Brennan

I'll never forget that call. It was my long time friend, Mary Kaye. The kind of friend where we could go without seeing each other for a long time, and yet when we picked up the phone, it was as though no time had passed.

What she said brought shivers through me.

"I've got a lump on my tongue the doctors are concerned about," she said. "Any thoughts?"

"Cat got your tongue?" I said immediately and a bit flippantly. "Anything you're holding back or not saying?"

"Like all my life!" She answered with a sigh.

And there it was. The repression of her self-expression had found a way to express itself.

"I'll let you know what they find out," she promised.

About a month later, I heard from her again. This time she sounded garbled, like she had a mouth full of marbles. But I understood her to say, "Well, they removed part of my tongue, but it still works!"

That was Mary Kaye. Always positive.

And always seeking more answers in life.

"I need your help," she said. "I have four tumors that don't look very good. I have my medical team of doctors who are going to do chemo and radiation. And I have my prayer team of my church, friends, and family. But I want you to be my energy team. And we have to come up with something different than what's out there because what's out there doesn't work!" She said clearly in spite of her partial tongue.

I immediately inwardly asked the angels, "Okay, what are we going to do?"

And I heard through my inner ears, "Don't worry. We've got this!"

So I said to Mary Kaye, "Don't worry. We've got this!"

"Good!" She said. "And another thing. I need a different word or phrase for what we're going to be doing because the terms the doctors use scare the be-jesus out of me."

So I turned to the angels and said, "Um, what are we going to call this?"

I heard, "Why, The Healing Angel Protocol, of course!"

I said to Mary Kaye, "How about The Healing Angel Protocol?"

"Perfect!" She said. And that's how it all began.

I asked the angels for meditations for her to use through her chemo and radiation. Guided meditations for self-healing. And I asked the angels for techniques when I didn't know what she needed.

And they came through with wonderful meditations and techniques.

At the end of four weeks, her four tumors had disappeared. That was the good news.

The bad news was that she now had a compromised liver and pancreas, and the doctors were making noises that she only had six months to live, at best.

But that didn't stop Mary Kaye. She posted on Facebook, showing off new clothes she had to get because she had lost so much weight, posting about how wonderful it was to go shopping for a size she hadn't seen since she was in high school, sharing photos of her grand-children and family, and having fun being with friends. Nothing was stopping her from enjoying life.

We continued doing sessions together, helping to clear fear, to step into wholeness and wellness, and to understand the physical, emotional, mental, and spiritual issues behind her illness. All the while, her body was so compromised, she had difficulty healing herself.

And when she did pass, she actually had lived longer than the doctors had predicted. And she left several legacies.

The first was her legacy of love. Everyone who came into her sphere of influence felt her unconditional love. You couldn't help but be affected by it. And this was her gift to all who knew her.

The second legacy was opening the door to the therapy, **The Healing Angel Protocol**™. Without her asking, I would never have talked to the angels about it. And without all the techniques we did together, I never would have felt inspired to offer them to other clients. Just to make sure these techniques worked on more people than just Mary Kaye. I never would have followed through on making this my legacy.

The techniques definitely worked on everyone I tried them on. And the angels brought more and more techniques and clients.

And suddenly, about a year after Mary Kaye had passed, I knew it was time to begin teaching the techniques to others. Within a year and a half, I had taught the six month Home Study Course several times, and added an advanced course of another three months.

Now besides the Home Study Course, there are trained practitioners, there's a webpage, there's an app called Healing with guided meditations, and I'm getting ready for the first ever Team Leader Training for those who will be doing the weekly calls on the Home Study Course. I have scheduled the 5 Day Live Immersion Training, some in Sedona, others elsewhere. And, of course, there's this book, *The Hollow Bone of Healing*.

Who could have predicted it would have exploded like this?

Only the angels. And the Quantum Field of Source Energy.

Next: The Basics

The Hollow Bone of Healing is not intended to replace conventional medical or psychological treatment. It is intended to be a complementary therapy. Always seek and follow the advice of your qualified medical or psychological practitioners. As a complementary therapy, it can have a huge impact on your physical, emotional, mental and spiritual health, without side effects. It does no harm.

The Basics

"Every step taken in mindfulness brings us one step
closer to healing ourselves and the planet."

~Thich Nhat Hanh

The Hollow Bone of Healing is a self-healing manual. The techniques outlined in this manual can help you restore your natural ability to heal yourself, achieve greater self-actualization, live a more peaceful and balanced life and are based on the therapy **The Healing Angel Protocol**™.

Specifically, these techniques can assist you as you

- release your old story and create a new one that better serves you
- restore your health to better balance by releasing old patterns and issues
- achieve any goal by overcoming your fears, and
- take inspired action toward your soul purpose

The therapy name **The Healing Angel Protocol**™ implies that you are only merging with angels. While certainly I have worked with angels all my life, and it's easy for me to connect with them when

I need help, when you access **The Healing Angel Protocol**™ and become The Hollow Bone of Healing, you are connecting with the Quantum Field of Source Energy, which contains all things. As you learn to connect to this field, you will discover all levels of consciousness and awareness. We hold the intention to only work with the highest and best for the client, the client's focus, and the requested healing. We simply don't have time to play with everyone, so we go for the highest and best.

Who you find at the top layer of the Quantum Field includes those aspects that are closest to source energy: angels, archangels, high level guides such as Jesus, Mother Mary, Buddha, deities, saints, and Spirits of Consciousness; such as The Spirit of Love, The Spirit of Light, The Spirit of Compassion, among others. Some of them you are familiar with and can know, sense, feel and recognize. Some are energies you are unfamiliar with. Sometimes you get a name for whom you are working with. Sometimes you don't.

One of the first things you will learn in the therapy **The Healing Angel Protocol**™ is how to perceive energy and consciousness. Part I of this manual will teach you simple ways you can interpret energy so you can trust the process, know you are connected to the highest and best, and see the intended results for your highest good and healing. And you'll learn what we mean by being The Hollow Bone of Healing, and ways to embody that for yourself.

Once you understand how you perceive energy and consciousness, Part II will give you four separate techniques to assist you with self-healing and being The Hollow Bone for miracles and messages.

This book is not just providing a modality or therapy to use when we're hurting, *The Hollow Bone of Healing* is a way of living. We utilize the techniques on a daily basis, so as to continue our self-actualization and to continue raising our consciousness.

When we raise our consciousness, we

- experience more daily harmony
- attract more kind and compassionate people in our lives
- quickly heal from physical, emotional, mental and spiritual traumas
- understand that that we are connected to a higher wisdom, higher knowledge, higher love and we act from those places
- experience more synchronicities in alignment with who we are and why we're here
- appreciate ourselves and others without judgment
- understand we can make a difference in the world through our own energetic shifts and so much more.

You don't have to be spiritual to benefit from either **The Healing Angel Protocol**™ or this book, *The Hollow Bone of Healing*. You don't have to be religious. Both are associated with the Quantum Field of Source Energy, which includes all things.

This book is for you if you are seeking complementary therapy that is new and different, that provides results at a deeper level, and is a way of living, not just a modality for today. It is for you if you haven't yet achieved the level of self-healing you are seeking.

And this book is for you if you are a practitioner of the healing arts and are intending to broaden your practice, help more people, and make a bigger difference in the world. The techniques here and in the therapy, **The Healing Angel Protocol**™, are perfect as stand-alone techniques or added to other complementary therapies.

Thank you for reading this and changing your life!

Next: Part I: How to Sense Energy and Be *The Hollow Bone of Healing*

Part I

How to Sense Energy and Be The Hollow Bone of Healing

CHAPTER ONE

How to Sense Energy

As human beings, we haven't lost our intuition; we just
stopped paying attention.

~Heidi DuPree,
The Other Medicine That Really Works

Background.

Have you ever walked into a room where someone just had an
argument, and you felt it? You noticed that something wasn't
quite right. Possibly you felt goose bumps, or tasted something
yucky in your mouth. Or noticed a jangling of your nerves without
visible cause. Maybe you even heard leftover words, either said
or unsaid. And it's even possible you could see "lines" of anger
in the room.

These are signs of energy.

Not everyone is aware of these signs. Most of the world is non-
energy aware and people travel through the day, without noticing
their sensations, feelings, or knowings. They miss cues from
source that indicate what they should pay attention to, whether
it's the energy of anger in a place where they don't choose to be,
or the energy of joy where they'd much rather be, or the energy of
consciousness that takes us to a higher wisdom, higher knowing.

Sometimes signs of energy are warnings, like having a "bad feeling" about traveling into a certain area or building. Sometimes energy signs are almost uplifting and giddy, as when we meet our special mate or partner. But if we don't know how we sense or how to interpret energy, we may miss these signs from the universe - which makes it harder to get our attention and makes life more difficult. Without understanding our signs, we can wander aimlessly without understanding why we feel lost. We can jump into hasty decisions without taking the time to sense if this possibility is the right thing for us. We can live mindlessly, instead of mindfully, without awareness of the effects on our bodies or our environment.

Our Senses

Probably ninety percent of the population is visual. When you think about it, our society is based on visually-appealing products, billboards, pictures, clothing, food - just about everything and all intending to reach out to you and draw you in. And for those ninety percent visual sensors, they *are* drawn in. They see and they react. For those who are energy sensitive, they also see with their inner eyes, meaning they sense objects, symbols, colors, or people that no one else is seeing.

Like the time I was sitting with a woman who was telling me about her husband who had recently passed. She said, "I just wish I could talk to him. I have something I'm worried about, and he was always able to help me."

At that moment, I saw him next to her. I didn't know her very well, so I didn't know him by sight, but I was totally aware that he was her husband, and he wasn't in the physical form. I just assumed she saw him too, so I said, "Well, he's right there. Why don't you just ask him?"

She stared at me for a moment, and then said, "What does he look like?"

I hesitated because he was wearing a really ugly yellow sweater with bright blue pants that didn't match, and I didn't want to say it that way. So I finally said, "Well, he has thinning light brown hair parted on one side, and is wearing a yellow sweater."

She looked at me, and then reached into her purse and drew out a picture of the very person I was seeing at that moment! Dressed in that horrible sweater and with thinning hair. I think both of us were speechless for a moment.

That's what I mean when I say "seeing with your inner eye."

But what about the rest of the world? The ten percent that isn't primarily visual. Which senses work best for them?

Well, first of all there is our largest organ, which is our skin. Yes, the skin is an organ. An organ is self contained and has a vital function. Our skin covers our bones, muscles and interior, and it functions as protection, regulation of body temperature and circulation, as well as sensation and detection of changes in the environment. Our skin reacts in goose bumps when we sense temperature or absolute truth. In other words, our skin can detect the presence of energy that is different from ours and either tightens or ripples. Our skin is a great receptor of energy. When was the last time you felt goose bumps?

I remember a time when my goose bumps were so large, that they felt like they were the size of cantaloupes. I was visiting an ancient site called Walnut Canyon in Arizona. It was a community ruin, meaning a large civilization had built their homes there, lived there at one time, and then left, without anyone knowing who they were, or why they disappeared. It was a very interesting area to explore, and afterward several of us had a picnic lunch on top of the canyon overlooking many of the ruins. We noticed that there was a structure by the picnic area that was covered, but appeared to be as old as the rest of the ruins. It was covered to the point where you could barely distinguish it. No visible signs around it indicated what it was. But when I looked at it, my goosebumps jumped out of my skin. Somehow I just knew it wasn't a happy place. It felt like a place of death and destruction, which contrasted deeply with the rest of the community. That night I had a dream about the structure and saw that inside it were lots of bones. It was actually like a deep well, and lots of people had been thrown in and killed. Either the Spanish or another warring culture had done this. And the spirits of those people had never been able to move on. They were the reason for the goosebumps. When I awoke I did a ceremony to help their spirits move to the light, and after that I didn't have any more goosebumps.

That's what I mean by the skin and goosebumps being dual receptors of changes in the environment.

Then there are our ears and our inner ears. Our physical ears can hear conversations, tones, frequencies, pitches, and so much more. And our inner ears can sense these at greater levels. When was the last time you heard a voice in your head warning you not to cross the street just then, or telling you to leave a building immediately? Our inner ears pick up so many subtle energy signs that we simply don't notice in any other way.

When I open my senses and merge with the Quantum Field of Source Energy, I usually hear voices talking to me. Angels, Archangels, and Spirits all have conversations with me. It makes me laugh when people talk about the voices in their heads because I have that all the time.

But these voices speak loving thoughts with compassion, and they never tell me to do anything that would be harmful. In fact, it was my ability to hear the angels that helped me to assist Mary Kaye, and to channel **The Healing Angel Protocol**™ course structure. I heard each Level being described, and as I got ready to teach, the angels would describe each module and what we were going to learn.

And that's what I mean by our inner and outer ears.

What about our taste buds? Have you tasted something really yucky when you didn't even have anything to eat? Or smelled something horrible where there was no visible source? These senses are here for us as well.

One time my partner, Leon, and I were hiking a new trail we'd read about. It sounded pretty magical, going back into the woods into a box canyon with ruins. We were hiking along, but something started happening to both of us. We walked more slowly, and something started to smell pretty horrible. It got worse and worse as we walked, and finally we stopped, practically gagging. I really thought I was going to throw up, as it smelled like something dead. I didn't know what we were going to find if we went on, and I really didn't think I could go forward. At that point, a couple came from behind us and looked at us curiously.

I asked without thinking, "Do you smell anything?" They just shook their heads and kept walking briskly.

Leon and I looked at each other as the smell got stronger and both of us said at the same time, "Let's get out of here!"

We left without making it to the end of the trail. That night we both had a dream where we were Native Americans being chased by soldiers on that trail. And we both died from being shot. When we woke up, we did a short ceremony to celebrate our lives and to help those aspects of our soul to move forward, and we never had that experience again.

That's what I mean by our sensors of taste and smell.

And then there's the knowing sense. The one where you just know *what* you know without knowing *how* you know. This is a tricky one because we don't have any visual, auditory, or sensory cues for it, so it can be difficult to trust. However, it's usually the most accurate. There is something to be said for "knowing it in your bones."

Like the time I had a sense I might die that day. I was sixteen and had a date that night. I was excited but I was also terrified because I kept having a sense, a knowing that something bad was going to happen, and I might die. When my date arrived, he brought me a long-stemmed red rose. He met my parents, and then we began walking to the car. I felt that sense of dread and fear rise up in my throat as I walked more slowly. Then I realized I'd forgotten to bring the rose with me! So I dashed back to the house, where my

Dad asked me a question about what time I expected to be back that night. I answered him, grabbed the rose, and ran back to the car. Suddenly that feeling, that knowing shifted, and I no longer felt the dread and fear. As we drove down the hill and turned the corner, here was a terrible accident that had just happened. A car had T-boned another car on the passenger side at that intersection.

I found out later it was a sixteen year old female passenger who died from that accident. And I knew it could have been me, had I not run back for the rose.

This is what I mean by knowing *what* you know without knowing *how* you know.

Of course we are so multi-sensory it's entirely possible we can have several senses all reporting to us at once! Confirming more easily what we are sensing in terms of energy.

So how do you sense energy? I have a free guided meditation available for you to listen to and help you to realize just how to open your senses to energy and what your strongest senses are. By knowing and opening your senses, you will have a stronger connection to the Quantum Field of Source Energy and be able to trust your experiences so you can receive miracles and messages all your life.

Access the Open Your Senses Meditation here. (Just use your best email address and create a new password.) https://phoenix-rising-star.mykajabi.com/offers/E8xyELD2

The Meditation: Our Senses

I invite you to find a place that's comfortable, where you can sit or lie down for twenty/twenty five minutes. As you do this, just center your awareness in your heart and allow your breathing to become slow and rhythmic at a rate that works for you. It's easy to entrain the body for relaxation and even transformation through the breath and through the heart.

(Silence)

We are about to open up all of our senses, and we're going to begin with your skin. Your skin is your largest organ and as such it has sensors everywhere. Your skin is actually very adept at sensing energy. You might have noticed having goose bumps in the past or chills or even hot flashes that might be angel flashes and not hormonal, and certainly there are other senses as well through your skin. As you turn your awareness to your skin, just allow your senses and your knowledge and awareness to open up and to experience what it's like to sense Source through your skin.

(Pause)

Feeling it. Knowing it. Understanding it. Confirmation comes through the skin many times. Just allow yourself to remember times when you felt and sensed through your skin.

(Silence)

Next, turn your awareness to your eyes but not your physical eyes. These would be your non-physical eyes. Some might call this your third eye. In addition to that eye, there are so many other non-physical eyes. Most of them are in the center of your forehead in a straight line, and there may be others. As you turn your awareness to your non-physical eyes, allow these eyes to sense energy. Energy can appear as colors or forms or light, maybe even symbols. With your intention, open your non-physical eyes to be aware of how you perceive energy in this way and just allow.

(Silence)

Next, turn your awareness to your nose to allow your sense of smell to help you remember things. Your sense of smell is very acute for remembrance and our connection to Source. Not only can you connect to maybe favorite relatives through the smell of baking or cinnamon or special cookies but you can connect to Source through the fragrance of flowers. Many times people will smell Rose, Jasmine, Lavender, Lily of the Valley, Lilacs and the list goes on.

With your intention, open up your olfactory sense, so that you can sense the presence of Source with your nose. It's very helpful to be able to smell Roses and to feel the love.

(Silence)

Turn your awareness to your sense of taste. There are so many ways in which our mouth and our tongue get our attention, sometimes through extra saliva, when things are really juicy or exciting, or through dryness of the mouth, when things become a little challenging. Plus we have all those taste sensations on our tongue; sweetness, sour, bitter and salty. Use your intention to open up your sense of taste, to allow yourself to sense and taste Source Energy in juicy bits, if it's appropriate for you.

(Silence)

Turn your awareness to your ears - but not your physical ears, your non-physical ears (those that allow you to hear tones or frequencies or signals not of the physical world, maybe even conversations that no one else hears). If you've had a persistent ringing of your ears, it may be Source Energy trying to get your attention. Just allow your ears, your non-physical ears, to open up and sense the beautiful tones of Source Energy.

(Silence)

Next, turn your awareness to your inner knowing on the inside of your body. This is the place where you just know what you know, without knowing how you know it. Most of the time it's somewhere in your core area, such as a gut feeling or in your heart, or somewhere in between. This sense can be the hardest to believe because it's so non-physical. But, it's actually very accurate once we trust it. So, just open up your inner knowing with your intention and allow yourself to receive messages in this way if it's appropriate for you.

(Silence)

Many people will experience Source with multiple senses, not just one. This actually gives you more confirmation. If you can sense it on your skin with goose bumps and maybe hear a tone and just know that it's the voice of an angel, that's pretty good confirmation. Just know that Source Energy will find the best ways to connect and communicate with you.

Now that you have opened up your senses, it will be so much easier, both for Source to connect with you, and for you to receive your guidance. Note that all of these senses send their vibrations and perceptions right to the heart, so that your heart can discern and interpret what is right for you. Honor what your heart is saying and know that you will continue to have a better connection, the more you continue to open your senses to Source. For now, just allow yourself to be held in loving vibrations as you allow all of your senses to be open to Source. You may even begin to receive more messages at this time. So just relax and enjoy, and stay here for as long as you like, long after the music is complete.

Reflection

- What I noticed about my sensing with....
- My Skin:
- My Eyes:
- My Nose:
- My Taste:
- My Ears:
- My Inner Knowing:
- An experience I had that surprised me:
- An experience I had that confirmed something to me:

Next: Part I: How to Sense Energy and Be the Hollow Bone of Healing Chapter Two: How to be The Hollow Bone of Healing

CHAPTER TWO

How to Be The Hollow Bone of Healing

"The Bat Phone to the Universe," some kind of Iva-only, open-round-the-clock special channel to the divine.

~Elizabeth Gilbert, *Eat, Pray, Love*

Background.

The Hollow Bone of Healing is actually a shamanic phrase, meaning being a pipeline to the divine. In our case, it is being a conduit or a channel for the Quantum Field of Source Energy. I call it the place of everything and the place of nothing. It is the place of everything because by being the conduit, Source Energy can do all the work of healing, miracles and bringing messages through us. We're not doing anything, but being a channel.

And it is also the place of nothing because we're not doing anything except being a channel. We don't have to move our arms, or follow any techniques because we're not doing the work. Source is. We could just sit there and not say anything or do anything, and messages, healing, and miracles would still happen. But that can be hard for people to understand. Sometimes we are guided to place our hands on people's heads or shoulders to help transmit energy.

Or if we're offering a distant session, we may be speaking more and sharing more messages.

So it's the place of everything where Source does all the work through us and the place of nothing because we have nothing to do with what happens. We simply hold the intention for the healing to be for the highest good and healing for all concerned. And it is.

I asked several of my students what it felt like to them to be The Hollow Bone of Healing.

My actual question to them was, "How do you know you're in your heart and/or how to you know how to move from your head to your heart to be The Hollow Bone?"

> Grace: "For me, I just said to myself, "Okay I trust that I'll be able to do the merge." And when I did that, it wasn't always the way you described it. But the way I kind of knew I was merged was that my whole body was vibrating, and there was this rush of energy like when you exercise a lot, and you get that huge rush of energy, and you just know that you are merging with a being of a higher nature because you feel your energy shift higher. The more you do it, the more you trust. It just takes time and practice."

> Eylah: "For me, I feel this sense of calmness and sensations in my body. But the minute I start thinking about it I lose the merge because I'm in my head. It's about trusting the process, and about being open. When I get in my head because I'm questioning, I just ask to go back into my heart. Sensations like tingles, vibrations, or warm chills tell me I'm in my heart."

> Lisa: "There's nothing to be afraid of. Nothing is going to harm you by doing this. Sometimes the merge seems to fill up your whole body, and sometimes it isn't quite that large. Whatever comes into your mind is a message, so take it. Write it down and then let that go."

Janel: "When I'm patient with myself, and I really feel that love, I feel the merge. And that's one of my biggest stumbling blocks is getting to that place, because I'm usually in a hurry to get there and do it. It's so easy when you lead us, but when I do it myself, it takes me longer to get there, and I get impatient. When I am the hollow bone, I don't have to search for what is to be shared, it just comes. Names just pop up. Information is just there."

Flo: "Usually for me, I can tell my helpers are there because I feel tingles all over. That tells me to pay attention. When I go into the hollow bone state, it's really peaceful and calm. And yeah, my brain has a tendency to pay attention to colors, trying to observe without getting in my own way. Usually it's calm and peaceful. Sometimes I'll feel some tears. Sometimes if I get too much in my head, I keep repeating, "Love, Gratitude, Hollow Bone" until I feel that energy flow again. When I'm in my head, I am wanting to see more or get more information, and that doesn't work. So the best for me is to just say, "Let me be the hollow bone, and I'll draw whatever they need." (Flo draws pictures of what she sees when offering a session as a practitioner.)

For me, when I'm The Hollow Bone of Healing, I feel so light and free. Since it begins with that sense of unconditional love, I feel that love, and I know I am loved and supported. I know I could just be present without doing anything at all, and everything will happen that needs to happen. The right messages will come through. The incredible miracles will take place, either visually or cellularly.

Such as the time I was offering ten minute sessions at an energy conference. A young man stepped up and asked for a session. I asked him, "How would you like your life to be different as a result of this session?"

He thought for a moment, then shrugged and said, "Release stress."

An angel stepped forward immediately and said to me, "No, we're working on his back." I said to him, "No, you've got an angel working on your back."

He looked at me rather strangely, but then shrugged and sat down.

I stepped into the state of love and became The Hollow Bone of Healing. I didn't know what was happening, but knew something was. I could feel energy moving up and down his spine. After ten minutes, the angel said, "We're done." And I told him we were finished.

He stood up, and I could see instantly he was about two inches taller than ten minutes ago. He grinned and threw a lot of money at me and left. The next day he came back and still looked straight and tall. This time he said, "My back is healed. I've had that all my life, and my back is healed." All in ten minutes. I'm not even sure what exactly happened or what he meant by saying his back was healed. But I knew I felt something. I knew an angel was doing something. And I could visually see he was taller and straighter.

Well, a miracle only takes a second.

The Hollow Bone of Healing is a place of observing without doing. Being present without doing.

Yes, I get tingles in my mid-section that indicate something is happening. But I don't have to know what that something is. I just trust that something is happening, and it is perfect for the person or situation. And the tingling will continue until the session is complete. At that point, the tingling dissipates, and I'm aware I have come back to my conscious awareness, while not being aware I ever left it.

It's definitely a process that begins with trusting that when you connect to the Quantum Field of Source Energy, you are connecting with the highest and best energy for the highest good and healing, and that who comes in is perfect for the session.

Next: Part II: The Self Healing Techniques while being The Hollow Bone of Healing. Chapter One: The Merge Technique

PART II

The Self-Healing Techniques while being The Hollow Bone of Healing

.

CHAPTER ONE

The Merge Technique, Steps One and Two

When we make the choice to fill our heart space with
unconditional love, our worlds blossom into a beauty
far greater than we have known.

~Rio Godfrey

The Background: Step One: Unconditional Love

Everything begins with Love. Love heals all things. Love is all things. When we act from a state of Love, our actions touch the heart of all involved. When we speak from a place of Love, our words are heard more often. When we create from a place of Love, our creations are for the highest good and healing for all concerned.

So we begin both the therapy **The Healing Angel Protocol**™ and this book *The Hollow Bone of Healing* from a state of love.

The kind of Love we refer to here is Unconditional Love. The kind of Love that doesn't judge, doesn't have restrictions or conditions around it, and is freely available whether you desire it or not.

No matter how you define Source. Whether you use the term God, Goddess, The One, The Universe, Source, and so on, it all means the same thing in my experience. So use the term you are most familiar with, that resonates the most with you, and the term that will help you open your heart to Unconditional Love.

Some of us have never experienced Unconditional Love. Maybe you grew up in a place where no one knew what it was and couldn't share it with you. Life was hard, and that's just how it was. Conditional love was the rule, as in 'do it this way and I'll love you. Don't do it this way and I won't.'

But sometimes we have found Unconditional Love in ways other than family.

Possibly, you were lucky enough to experience Unconditional Love with a favorite pet or animal, feeling and knowing and sensing that adoration that came from the shared loyalty.

Maybe you have sensed Unconditional Love in a place in nature where you felt connected to all life everywhere. Hiking in the wilderness, where there are only plants, trees, animals, water, soil and your own thoughts can really bond you to all life everywhere, helping you to feel calm and centered and connected.

You might even have been lucky enough to have a relationship with an unrelated person who never judged you and always offered you Love, whether you accepted it or not. Rather like serving cookies on a platter, "Here have some if you like," without expectation or discrimination.

We're all different in our experiences, so do the best you can do with Unconditional Love. I can promise you that it will get easier the more you practice. Remember, this is not just a technique or a modality. This is a way of living. And this is a process you'll want to practice daily to keep your inspiration high, your heart open, and the miracles flowing.

All techniques in the therapy **The Healing Angel Protocol**™ and in this book are based on Unconditional Love and The Merge. So we begin everything by staying in that loving state for some time, as it nurtures and supports us.

Just in case you are feeling triggered by your past experiences, I have included as a bonus, an extra guided meditation to help you clear and heal those triggers. It is called The Clearing Meditation, and you can access it here any time: **https://phoenix-rising-star.mykajabi.com/offers/E8xyELD2**

Background: Step Two: The Merge Process

From this state of love, it's then easy to hold the intention for connecting with the highest and best consciousness in the Quantum Field of Source Energy, for the highest good and healing of all concerned.

Let me make it clear that you are not going to merge with the entire Quantum Field of Source Energy. From a state of love, you are opening the door to the field and asking, "Who is the highest and best for this situation?" And you're accepting who comes in.

Whoever accepts the request may be a familiar saint, deity, angel, archangel, or ascended master. Or it may be a high consciousness spirit such as The Spirit of Love, The Spirit of Light, The Spirit of Compassion. It also may be a high level spirit you have never encountered before, but you will be asked to sense their essence with your heart to see if it feels right. If it feels right, it is right. If it doesn't feel right, end the session, and continue to stay in that state of Unconditional Love. Just know that you really will connect with who is the highest and best for all concerned.

Using all of your senses to see, sense, hear, and know whom you are connecting with.

Feel the wave of Love, that Unconditional Love that heals all things, that comes to you from your helper, and that surrounds you and supports you. Allow yourself to receive it and send it back, feeling the wave of Love build and build between you.

Staying in a state of giving and receiving Love with your spirit helper, helps establish trust, and helps you open yourself to being The Hollow Bone of Healing.

When that mutual Love has been established, you'll know it because it's a place of calm support, rather like being wrapped in cotton wool. Safe, loving, warm.

And at that point you can ask to merge your frequency entirely with this high level being.

There are different definitions for what I call The Merge. There's the shamanic term for "transmutation," meaning releasing the ego and stepping into the divine essence. There's the religious term, "transfiguration," meaning to change your appearance into a more beautiful or miraculous state. And then there's what I call The Merge, which is to merge your energy field entirely with that of your spirit helper.

Basically what they all have in common is to be The Hollow Bone of Healing, release all thoughts of controlling the outcome, and open your heart to the Source of All Things to connect through you for your highest good and healing.

There are three simple methods for merging.

One. Just holding the intention for merging or transfiguring is enough, and it will happen very easily, gently and lovingly.

Two. As you feel the wave of Love between you and your spirit helper, when you are ready, your helper will move behind you so you are now feeling that wave of Love coming into the back of your heart. When invited, your helper will move its energy forward into and through the back of your heart, merging your energies together entirely. Rather like slipping on a glove, one finger at a time. You might have sensations of light pressure or opening in your back area, but you might not.

Three. As you feel the wave of Love between you and your spirit helper, when you are ready, your helper will merely step forward so it is in front of you as you continue to feel that wave of Love coming into your heart. When invited, your helper will continue to move its energy into your heart, merging your energies together entirely. You might experience sensations of light pressure or tension or expansiveness or anything else or nothing else.

Choose the method you think will work best for you and try it out. If you don't feel you have success, try a different method.

Merging your frequency with this higher Consciousness, higher Love, higher Wisdom, higher Knowing is enough to create change into a more beautiful or miraculous state and offer messages, healing and miracles.

And it feels so good, you'll want to stay in that place forever.

When you are merged, you will be ready to receive messages in the ways that are right for you. Hearing words or sounds, seeing pictures, people, symbols, colors, smelling or tasting memories or new information, feeling goosebumps, or knowing without knowing how you know.

It's also possible you will receive whatever healing is for your highest good. Again, using all your senses, you may feel things, sense things, know things or experience things. You may be two inches taller at the end of your session. You may not. You may attract the perfect partner immediately. Or in your divine timing. You may achieve financial freedom - now or in the future. Whatever you receive can happen within twenty-four to forty-eight hours or in its divine timing. And it will be whatever is for your highest and best, because that's what we asked for. We may not know what that means when we ask for it. But we will know it when we experience it. A change in Consciousness means there's a change somewhere.

Stepping into The Hollow Bone of Healing by staying in a place of Unconditional Love. It is the place of no thought, and no mind, just heart. It is the place of everything and the place of nothing. Peaceful. Calm. Knowing everything. Being everything. Just being.

You are staying there until it's time to come back. You'll know when that is because the energy just kind of dissipates. Maybe it's not feeling as strong, or as tingly. Or maybe the messages stop. Or the images cease. Or the sounds change and disappear. Or maybe you just know you're complete for now.

Coming back to your consciousness, just stay there for a few minutes in silence to integrate what you experienced. Integration is a key piece for understanding and trying to put into words what you experienced. Words help us ground our experience into reality, and make it easier to experience another time. You might want to journal your experience or record your experience. Maybe do this with a trusted friend where you can share your experiences to make it more real.

The first time you do The Merge, use the Free Guided Meditation for The Merge. It takes you through this process step by step, so you can embody that state of Love, merge with an aspect of Source Energy, step into The Hollow Bone of Healing where you are everything and you are nothing, and then come back transformed with miracles, messages, and healing. It's so much easier to listen and follow along, than to try to do this alone at first. Once you get the idea and have mastered the technique, you can do this on your own without the meditation. (Remember what Janel said? "When you lead us, it's so much easier!")

When I first experienced The Hollow Bone of Healing, I had been facilitating **The Healing Angel Protocol**™ for awhile. I had been merging, facilitating messages, healing and miracles, and really felt like I understood it. But the day came when I merged and all of a sudden, it was as though I couldn't move my arms, I couldn't open my mouth, I really couldn't do anything. All I could do was observe. And I 'saw' with my inner eyes that Archangel Michael was working with the DNA in my client's spine. It was as though he pulled it out like ticker tape, running his hands over it, up and down. Cleaning it as though wiping away any debris with his thumb and forefinger as they moved up and down. Then he put it back in and announced to me, "So let the client know her DNA is now cleared of old ancestral patterns that weren't hers. And that now she is freer to move forward and manifest what she chooses, not more of the same limiting pattern."

I told my client that. She mentioned feeling something in her spine, but also mentioned a feeling of lightness and freedom she'd never had before. And spoke of wanting to purchase a new car, which she had never had in her life. Consequently, she bought one the next week. I mentioned to my students later that I had never done anything so easy in my life because I did nothing. I was simply The Hollow Bone of Healing - at a depth I'd never experienced before. I believe that the more you do this work, the more infinite you find it to be, and the more miracles are possible to receive.

Access your FREE Guided Meditation, The Merge, here: https://phoenix-rising-star.mykajabi.com/offers/E8xyELD2

The Meditation: How to Merge.

Just close your eyes and turn your awareness to your heart, to your energetic heart space that is located behind your literal heart. This is the place that holds the sacred space of your heart, the tiny space of your heart that only you know about. That holds all of your records for being and all of your lifetimes, all of your goals, your aspirations, your lessons, your teachings. Everything is stored there, and not just for you, but for all life. So, we hold gratitude for being aware of that and knowing how to access it, as I invite you to also begin generating feelings of Unconditional Love.

(Silence)

And sometimes you might have a chant or a mantra that you say to get you into this space like, "Love, Gratitude, Hollow Bone." Or you may have your own mantra that you might say. Or maybe you have a memory of a beautiful experience with a two-legged or four-legged, in which you just felt so much Unconditional Love. Or possibly you have had an experience with Source Energy, a straight direct experience with Source, in whatever way you define Source. Maybe you were out in nature and you just felt at one and at peace with all life everywhere.

(Silence)

So, whatever it is that will help you to embody more Love, just allow yourself to be in that space and to allow all of that Love to begin filling up your heart space, both your energetic and your physical space. Filling up kind of like water fills up a container. As it pours in, it fills from the bottom to the top, and as that Unconditional Love continues to flood in, what happens is the Unconditional Love floods out of your heart space and begins filling up your physical form. Again, just like a container, from the bottom to the top. So, from the bottoms of your feet, filling up every cell in your body with this Unconditional Love, and with no place hiding from this love.

(Silence)

Really feeling that, and letting it fill up all the way to the top until it overflows into your physical energetic layer of your energy field. Again, filling from the bottom to the top, and hiding no place from this Love. Each layer that gets filled, you just start feeling kind of like some padding is being added to you, and this wonderful, loving material is just being wrapped around you like cotton gauze. It's soft, and it's warm, and it's comforting. Most of all it's loving.

(Silence)

And then it spills over into your emotional layer, and again you're filling up from the bottom to the top, adding just another layer of this wonderful Unconditional Love that is wrapping all around you, making you feel so comfortable and at peace and at one, loved and supported.

(Silence)

Spilling over into your mental energetic layer, filling up from the bottom to the top. Knowing that you are loved and supported and healing any belief systems that would be in the way of knowing this.

(Silence)

Filling up until that spills over into your spiritual layer, which also encompasses your light body. This is a very vast layer, and may take a little bit longer to fill up with Unconditional Love because it is so big. But again, hide no place from this Love. When this is full, this is a beautiful place to be, and it's perfect to just sit for a moment or two, and just be there. Be this Love. This is the beginning of The Hollow Bone of Healing. There isn't anything you have to do. You are so deeply and profoundly connected in that Unconditional Love that feeling and being that Love is all that matters. Just feel that, know that, and be that.

(Silence)

From this place, you may invite in the presence of that who is the highest and best for this session. You may see, sense, or know in some way, or just intend that you are connecting heart-to-heart, feeling that wave of Love that is being sent to you. Really allow yourself to receive this, and take this into every layer. When you're complete, send it back, and know that this Love is being received. It's very important to your helper to feel your Love.

(Silence)

And as your helper takes it in, Love is magnified about ten times before your helper sends it right back to you. Now, allow yourself to open your heart and really receive all this, gratefully, with appreciation, with more Love. And, when you send it back, know it's being received.

(Silence)

One last time, this Love is multiplying to the nth degree and then being sent back to you, and you are feeling this wave of Love between you that is almost beyond human understanding. So, just feel that and be that for a moment.

(Silence)

When you're ready, you can merge entirely with your helper's energy using any of the methods that appeal to you. It's now really easy to be together, and during this time you may receive messages, you may receive some healing, or you may just be in that energy. Open all your senses, step into The Hollow Bone of Healing, and just allow whatever is for your highest and best to happen. Seeing, sensing, feeling, knowing whatever is best for you right now.

[Silence]

It is enough by merging with your helper to open the door to miracles.

[Silence]

At some point, that will feel very complete. You will know it. You'll sense that there is nothing more that needs to be said, done or achieved because it is all there. You have done what you were asked to do, and you did it well.

So, at this point, your helper will step aside from the merge, but you'll still feel this wonderful Love. The feelings will dissipate. The intensity will calm. And the Love remains.

When that feels complete for now, you can gently bring yourself back into your body, back into the room.

Reflection

- I was able to step into Unconditional Love in this way:
- I experienced The Hollow Bone of Healing in this way:
- I experienced a being who was for my highest and best in this way, using my senses:
- I merged using this technique:
- The messages and/or healing I received appeared in this way:

Next: Part II: The Self-Healing Techniques Chapter Two: The Time-Space Continuum

Want to experience merging to help others, and even the environment?

Excited to work with plant spirits and mineral sprits for messages and healing?

Check out our website: HealingAngelProtocol.com for more information on Take the Training! Classes are continually being added and updated, so check back often!

PART II

The Self-Healing Techniques while being The Hollow Bone of Healing

CHAPTER TWO

The Time-Space Continuum

> This research reminds us that we hold many of the levers
> of healing in our own hands. It makes us aware that it is
> not doctors, hospitals, acupuncturists, homeopaths, chi-
> ropractors, energy workers, or other health professionals
> who determine our sickness and health. They can tilt the
> balance, but not nearly as much as we can. Each of us,
> as individuals, creates a big chunk of our emotional and
> mental environment, thereby turning genes on and off in
> our cells. This opens up vast and exciting potential.
>
> ~ Dawson Church, *The Genie in Your Genes*

Background: What is Cell Memory and Cell Level Clearing?

Have you ever rubbed your forehead while trying to remember something? Or experienced tenderness or tightness in the back of your neck when a co-worker exploded on you?

These are examples of cellular memory areas, the map of our body that holds specific memories. Cellular memory, unlike the memory of your brain, stores experiences rather than just facts and figures. Experiences tend to be stored as impressions and are viewed from all senses, not just the visual. For example, the brain, when retrieving a memory will most likely show you a picture or a list or a graphic. Cells, when retrieving a memory will give you a body sensation such as pain or tension or tingling or you may be "frozen with fear". You may also sense a fragrance, taste, sound, or any combination of senses that held the imprint of the experience.

For example, when we experience trauma, no matter if it's real or perceived, we store those memories in our cells. Physically, we can store the pain, abuse, surgery, and so on. Emotionally we can store fear, worry, guilt, and more. Mentally, we store the conscious and unconscious beliefs formed around the trauma, such as 'I'm not good enough', 'I am unlovable', or 'Men are not safe'.

Unless we understand how to clear them, these cell memories then color our attraction factor to attract more of the same experiences. The Law of Attraction is a very powerful magnet that attracts to us exactly what we are broadcasting through our energy field. If we have abuse in our cell memories, we will attract more abuse, until we clear it from within. If we have positive beliefs that we are loveable, we will attract more of that.

Not everyone agrees that cellular memory exists. Scientists doubt it because there isn't a way to effectively measure it. Unlike brain waves and stimulation, cellular memory does occur in all cells, but there's no proof that the memory is actually stored there.

Some researchers, though, are beginning to put forth ideas that support cellular memory. Think back to the basic conditioned response as developed and observed by Pavlov. Ringing a bell produced salivation when paired with food initially. Thereafter, salivation happened with only the bell for association. Stimulation produced a bodily response, a sensory response, a muscle memory response to an event.

One of the more interesting people who scientifically studied the body in relation to the energy flow within it and the subsequent imprinting of cellular memory was Wilhelm Reich. In his work on character analysis, he focused on the conflicts of the ego. He saw the body divided by armor rings (cell memory energy blocks) that he described as being at right angles to one's spine. He perceived that these rings blocked the flow of what he called Orgon Energy (Life Force Energy). One develops these rings - this armor - from the energy products (such as guilt) from the ego. When one is blocked from the free flow of energy, one can outwardly express this blockage through anger or rage.

Post traumatic stress syndrome (PTSD) also relates to cellular memory. Survivors of stress or trauma exhibit multiple signs of ongoing memory in their bodies, such as

- physical symptoms such as shaking, inability to move or act, sweating
- emotional symptoms such as sadness, fear or anger
- mental symptoms such as aggression, inability to decide, powerlessness

These multiple senses are operating from traumatic events stored in the cellular memory.

Set points are another example of cellular memory. These points can control the comfort level of the body or mind with certain activities such as weight loss or gain, meditation length, endurance training, or giving/receiving abundance. These set points can be reconditioned or reset in the body and mind, allowing for greater loss or gain. In effect, you are retraining your neurons to fire at different times or places.

Vaccines can also be viewed as cellular memory. Regardless of how you feel about vaccines, look at the way they are supposed to work. You are given a shot that contains a small amount of an unhealthy organism. Your immune system sets up a counter-offensive to keep you from getting sick from it. Then your immune system "remembers" that type of experience to keep you healthy. Therefore, vaccines evoke cell memory by their actions.

Then there's the example of the organ donors and their recipients, reports come most frequently from heart transplant recipients. In one case, the donor wrote poetry and lyrics and in one unpublished poem he wrote about Danny who would receive his heart when he died. The recipient of his heart was Danielle who when the donor's parents talked to her about the poetry, found she could finish the lines of most of it without having any previous conscious knowledge of it. Then there's the police officer killed in an undercover drug deal. His heart was received by a man who kept reporting he saw flashes of light and felt a burning over his face. The police officer had been shot in the face.

There's also the study of epigenetics, which include the experiences, beliefs, and other imprints from our ancestors that prove we pass on more than just the color of our eyes and hair. If our grandparents experienced a traumatic event, chances are you have that stored in your DNA, and it can prevent you from living your joy just by its existence. Studies of holocaust survivors indicate their children begin experiencing PTSD at the same age their parents were when entering the concentration camps. The children experienced their parents' trauma without having even been born at that time!

Clearing and Healing at the Cell Level

So where is this going? If it's true that cellular memory exists, then why not facilitate healing at that level? If it's true that suppressing these memories can lead to disease and keep us from our joy, then why not heal at this level?

One plausible reason we aren't healing at this level is that the memories are suppressed, and we therefore don't even know we're holding onto them.

A good example of this is something that happened to me when I was twelve. Walking down a safe street, I saw a man approaching me. He was wearing a plaid shirt, blue jeans, and work boots, and was carrying a large stick. As he got closer, I felt intense fear without any known reason. I broke into a cold sweat and my feet became planted where I was, unable to move. I tasted the tang of fear in my throat and was unable to speak. I felt I was close to dying, and when he finally passed by me uneventfully I was able to break loose of my fear state and run home. When I got there, I told my Mom about the event.

Mom replied, "Oh honey, don't you remember?"

And at that moment, it all flooded back to my brain memory. My aunt had been kidnapped when I was 2 years old. I was present at the time the man, wearing a plaid shirt, blue jeans and work boots, broke into the house. He carried a sawed-off shot gun and threatened to kill everyone there. He demanded money and when he got it, grabbed my aunt and kidnapped her. She was later released physically unharmed. Because I was so young, I suppressed the mental memory but the cellular memory imprints of fear, tension, worry, and potential death stayed with me until I was able to release them successfully. My cellular memory retained the experiential impressions that I was able to understand at the time: the clothing, the big stick, the threatening behavior. After releasing that memory, I never again felt that level of fear when viewing plaid shirts or men with sticks! This is a simplified version of also saying that I never again felt unrelated fear to strange men approaching me on the street.

As "healers" or "facilitators of healing" as we prefer to be called, we see evidence of cellular memory all the time, especially when it's being released. Although this is purely observational and anecdotal and has no way of being measured empirically or proved that it's coming from anywhere other than the brain and the body, there's no doubt to us or the clients that it is coming from the basic cells themselves.

Physical evidence of cellular memory release is demonstrated by body movement, twitching, pulsing, feelings of twinges or tingling, even in areas where we aren't working. Even body miracles take place here as demonstrated by blood pressure decrease, blood sugar decrease, pain decrease or pain elimination, or other physical healing.

Emotional evidence of cellular memory release is shown through crying, laughing, talking, but not necessarily re-experiencing. **Through intention, it is possible to release cell memory without having to re-experience it. Therefore trauma does not have to be re-experienced in order to let it go.** This concept makes cell-level clearing profoundly different from traditional therapies.

Mental evidence of cellular memory release is shown through verbal processing, where connections are made that weren't visible before. People will change mental thought patterns that no longer serve them, and suddenly find themselves with patterns that are more helpful. They may release beliefs around having too much money and the possible negative connotations with that. And through realizing that, they are able to adopt a more beneficial attitude, such as money can be used any way you like. There's nothing evil about it. And again, it's also possible to release without knowing what it is you are releasing.

Spiritual evidence of cellular memory release is demonstrated by elimination of judgment toward oneself and others, a release of guilt and events by past life recall and connections to current situations. There is a stronger connection to all that is, or Source Energy, and a belief that it's not necessary to know where you are going, so long as you know you are on your way.

True cell level clearing and healing isn't just about releasing the memories stored there. It's also about replacing that memory with higher frequencies. When we release things, a vacuum is created, and unless we fill up that vacuum with a higher vibration, the same old pattern will be attracted back into the body. So as heartache is released for example, the cell level healing replaces that memory with a higher frequency of Source Essence. As guilt is released, cell level healing replaces that memory with the higher frequency of Source Essence. Source Essence means different things to different people. It can be experienced as Love, Peace, Comfort, and so much more.

How do we know that true cell level clearing is happening?

Again, this is observational and anecdotal. We see in our clients that they look lighter, freer, younger, more youthful and more empowered. They report this also. They say they feel and look like they've had a facelift without any of the side effects! They feel like they've lost ten pounds in one hour! **It feels this way because we don't realize how much energy it takes to hold onto suppressed memories.** It's only when we release the memories and feel how much more energy is now able to come through us that we make this connection.

And it's by connecting with Love and merging with the perfect helper from the Quantum Field of Source Energy that this can happen so easily and gently. Love is the foundation for everything we do within the therapy **The Healing Angel Protocol**™and this book.

This is the process of the Time-Space Continuum. Again beginning in a state of unconditional love, we ask to merge with whoever is for the highest and best for the client. That helper will point out the 'hot spots' within the energy field that are actually activated cellular memory spots preventing us from moving forward with ease and grace. Usually the 'hot spots' have something to do with the past, either ours or our ancestors. And they are activating now because the client is doing something similar that caused the 'hot spot' to become cellular memory initially. Once the 'hot spots' have been noticed, and the helper has shared messages through your sensing, feeling, or knowing, then Love is sent to the 'hot spot' to dissipate it until it is gone.

For example, I was having lunch with a friend. She was discussing the new book she was writing. She happened to mention running into a minor road block that was preventing her from finishing a chapter and knowing where to go next. I suddenly "saw" with my inner eyesight, a red fuzzy ball just above her right shoulder and knew instantly it was a "hot spot". I mentioned it to her, as she was someone familiar with **The Healing Angel Protocol**™ and asked her if she wanted it removed.

She said, "Yes!"

So I quickly stepped into that state of Love, merged with a helper from the Quantum Field of Source Energy, and the helper sent Love to it until it dissipated.

All of this happened during lunch, in a public place, and no one observed anything.

How? Because again, I did nothing. Source Energy did it all. All I did was become The Hollow Bone of Healing.

Later she mentioned going home after lunch and writing two more chapters.

When we merge for healing cellular memory, these "hot spots" can appear anywhere. And different ones will appear depending on what is activated, or what is going on in our lives at the time. So it's possible that every session is completely different, either needing the Time-Space Continuum of healing "hot spots" or not.

It's called the Time-Space Continuum because these "hot spots" come through time and space and as they are related to cellular memory, they can get activated at any time there is similarity in actions, choices, decisions, and soul purpose. They could be from a lifetime nine centuries ago, or from your grandparents' experiences.

What your helper does is point them out to you in a way that you can see, sense, feel or know where and what they are, to the best of your ability.

Then they simply send Love to the "hot spot" until it dissipates. The space of that cellular memory is then filled with Source Essence, which can mean different things for different people. For some it's the Essence of Peace. For others it's the Essence of Empowerment.

For still others it can be the Essence of Unconditional Love. It's different for different people and different cellular memories, but it's always perfect.

Remember that everything begins with Love, so the first part of this meditation may sound familiar. All the techniques in the therapy **The Healing Angel Protocol**™ and this manual begin with love.

Access your FREE Meditation for Healing the Time-Space Continuum here: https://phoenix-rising-star.mykajabi. com/offers/E8xyELD2

The Meditation: The Time-Space Continuum Healing

Just close your eyes and turn your awareness to your heart, to your energetic heart space that is located behind your literal heart. This is the place that holds the sacred space of your heart, the tiny space of your heart that only you know. That space holds all of your records for being and all of your lifetimes, all of your goals, your aspirations, your lessons, your teachings. Everything is stored there, and not just for you, but for all life. So, we hold gratitude for being aware of that and knowing how to access it, as I invite you to also begin generating feelings of Unconditional Love.

(Silence)

And sometimes you might have a chant or a mantra that you say to get you into this space like, "Love, Gratitude, Hollow Bone." Or you may have your own mantra that you might say. Or maybe you have a memory of a beautiful experience with a two-legged or four-legged, in which you just felt so much Unconditional Love. Or possibly an experience with Source Energy, a straight direct experience with Source, in whatever way you define Source. Maybe you were out in nature and you just felt at one and at peace with all life everywhere.

(Silence)

So, whatever it is that will help you to embody more Love, just allow yourself to be in that space and to allow all of that Love to begin filling up your heart space, both your energetic and your physical space. Filling up kind of like water fills up a container. As it pours in, it fills from the bottom to the top, and as that Unconditional Love continues to flood in, what happens is that the Unconditional Love floods out of your heart space and begins filling up your physical form. Again, just like a container, from the bottom to the top. So, from the bottoms of your feet, filling up every cell in your body with this Unconditional Love, and hiding no place from this Love.

(Silence)

Really feeling that, and letting it fill up all the way to the top until it overflows into your physical energetic layer of your energy field. Again, filling from the bottom to the top, and hiding no place from this Love. Each layer that gets filled, you just start feeling kind of like some padding is being added to you as this wonderful, loving material is just being wrapped around you like cotton gauze. It's soft, and it's warm, and it's comforting. It's loving.

(Silence)

And then it spills over into your emotional layer, and again you're filling up from the bottom to the top, adding just another layer of this wonderful Unconditional Love wrapping all around you, making you feel so comfortable and at peace and at one, loved and supported.

(Silence)

Spilling over into your mental energetic layer, filling up from the bottom to the top. Knowing that you are loved and supported and healing any belief systems that would be in the way of knowing this.

(Silence)

Filling up until that spills over into your spiritual layer, which also encompasses your light body. This is a very vast layer, and may take a little bit longer to fill up with Unconditional Love because it is so big. But again, hide no place from this love. When this layer is full, you'll find it a beautiful place to be, and it's perfect to just sit for a moment or two, and just be there. Be this Love. This is the beginning of The Hollow Bone of Healing. There isn't anything you have to do. You are so deeply and profoundly connected in that Unconditional Love that that's all that matters. Just feel that, know that, and be that.

(Silence)

From this place, you may invite in the presence of that who is the highest and best for this session. You may see, sense, or know in some way, or just intend that you are connecting heart-to-heart, feeling that wave of Love that is being sent to you. Really allow yourself to receive this, and take this into every layer. When you're complete, send it back, and know that this Love is being received. It's very important to your helper to feel your Love.

(Silence)

And as your helper takes it in, Love is magnified about ten times before your helper sends it right back to you. Now, allow yourself to open your heart and really receive all this, gratefully, with appreciation, with more Love. And, when you send it back, know it's being received.

(Silence)

One last time, this Love is multiplying to the nth degree and then being sent back to you, and you are feeling this wave of Love between you that is almost beyond human understanding. So, just feel that and be that for a moment.

[Silence]

When you're ready, you can merge entirely with your helper's energy using any of the methods that appeal to you. It's really easy to be together, and during this time you may receive messages, you may receive some healing, or you may just be in that energy. Open all your senses, step into The Hollow Bone of Healing, and just allow whatever is for your highest and best to happen. Seeing, sensing, feeling, knowing whatever is best for you right now.

[Silence]

It is enough by merging with your helper to open the door to miracles.

[Silence]

With all your senses open, be aware of what you are seeing, sensing, feeling and knowing. Open your heart to that Unconditional Love and your helper and allow your helper to share with you any "hot spots" within your Time-Space Continuum. You may feel them, see, them, know them, hear them, or you may have a combination of your senses to heighten your awareness. Allow yourself to be aware of these "hot spots" and notice if you receive any messages around them from your helper.

(Long Silence)

When any messages are complete, your helper will simply share Unconditional Love with these "hot spots" until they dissipate completely, helping you to feel freer, lighter, younger, and more focused.

(Long Silence)

And when that feels complete for now, your helper will disengage from The Merge and you can bring yourself back into your body and back into your room.

Reflection

- I was able to feel Unconditional Love in this way:
- My spirit helper from the quantum field was:
- I became aware of the (#) of hot spots in this way:
- My messages about them included:

Next: Part II: The Self-Healing Techniques Chapter Three: The Sphere of Manifesting. The clearer you are, the easier it is to manifest.

Want to know more about the twenty plus newly discovered cellular memory areas in the energy field and how to heal them? Check out Take the Training in our website, HealingAngelProtocol.com. Level I is the prerequisite for this Level II training on Healing Trauma.

PART II

The Self-Healing Techniques while being The Hollow Bone of Healing

CHAPTER THREE

The Sphere of Manifesting

When you have clarity and commit to manifesting your heart's desire, you will be drawn to those who light you up on every level...and they will be drawn to you.

~ Annette Vaillancourt, *How to Manifest Your Soulmate with EFT: Relationship as a Spiritual Path*

Background: The Sphere of Manifesting.

In Level III of the therapy **The Healing Angel Protocol**™, we access the sacred geometry of our energy field, the natural sacred geometry that is already within you, but may not be activated.

Sacred geometry is a phrase meaning any form or shape that opens your heart.

When we activate these shapes, they open our hearts to more Unconditional Love, to the balance of masculine and feminine energy, to the understanding of our third dimensional universe that we live in, and to moving our consciousness to a higher level, a higher plane of existence that helps us evolve as souls.

Sounds heavy, doesn't it?

It isn't as difficult as it may seem at first. We just take it one step at a time.

We learn and re-connect with the basic shapes and information systems in Metatron's Cube. Metatron's Cube is known all over the world as holding the building blocks to the universe. It holds all the platonic solids plus additional complex shapes.

A platonic solid is a simple shape that is defined in this way: all its angles are identical, all edges are identical, all faces are identical, and the entire solid fits on the face of a sphere.

There are only five of these in our world: the tetrahedron, the cube, the octahedron, the icosahedron, and the dodecahedron. Each of them represents a different element: fire, earth, air, water, and ether.

Surrounding Metatron's Cube is normally a sphere, sometimes called the sphere of influence. It contains all sacred geometry within itself.

What I have found is that Metatron's Cube and the Platonic Solids and the other geometries we study all have one thing in common: they all developed from a sphere.

The sphere is the beginning of creation. It is the birth of all new creations. The sphere is the egg. And this sphere is where all sacred geometry comes from.

No one has mentioned that until now. When I say no one, I mean none of the well known teachers of sacred geometry in the last fifty years. Possibly our ancient ancestors knew it, but they aren't saying.

So when we begin with the sphere, we are studying the heart of our creation, the basis of our next manifestation. And beginning with a sphere allows us to create from the very beginning, building a foundation of our dreams and wishes and taking them into reality.

And it's a lot easier than you might think, because you're already surrounded by a sphere called your energy field.

All we're going to do is tap into that shape and tap into your dreams to help you create your intention and get a sense of what your heart desires. We will be helping you to be open to your inspired action and create this reality now.

When we do this, you'll get a sense of your energy field in a sphere around you. Seeing it, sensing it, feeling it, knowing it. And then allow your dreams to enter in: the ones you remember, the ones you forgot, the ones that are most important for this time in your life, for where you are right now.

Because you have cleared your energy field of what might be in the way, you are now ready for this dream—creating a life of miracles and messages--to come true.

When I first connected with the sphere of influence through my energy field, I was surprised at all the dreams that came in. Dreams I had fulfilled. Dreams I was holding onto. Dreams I'd forgotten about. Dreams not quite complete. When that happens, it is simply an opportunity to ask yourself, what is best for me now?

So I stepped into a state of Love. I merged with my helper from the Quantum Field of Source Energy. And I asked that question: what is best for me now?

I was so blown away by the answer. Not that I was surprised by the content. I was dumbfounded by the depth of the answer, by the breadth of the answer, by the extent of my dream in ways I never thought or realized before.

The Healing Angel Protocol™ became a movement in my dreams. One that offers Love and Support to all life everywhere. As a result, it became the Home Course Structure and so much more. The Five Day Live Immersion. The Healing app of guided meditations. This book. The advanced courses. The Practitioners. The Team Leaders. The continual community support with planetary healing. Continual community support through channeled messages that empower and teach. It was and is so much bigger than I ever dreamed. And it all began with the sphere.

And within eighteen months, it was so. With more to come.

When you are ready to claim your dreams and manifest them into reality, listen to this meditation on The Sphere of Manifesting.

Remember that everything begins with Love, so the first part of this meditation may sound familiar. All the techniques in the therapy **The Healing Angel Protocol**™ and this manual begin with Love.

Access your Free Guided Meditation: The Sphere of Manifesting here: https://phoenix-rising-star.mykajabi.com/offers/E8xyELD2

Meditation: The Sphere of Manifesting.

Just close your eyes and turn your awareness to your heart, to your energetic heart space that is located behind your literal heart. This is the place that holds the sacred space of your heart, the tiny space of your heart that only you know. That space holds all of your records for being and all of your lifetimes, all of your goals, your aspirations, your lessons, your teachings. Everything is stored there, and not just for you, but for all life. So, we hold gratitude for being aware of that and knowing how to access it, as I invite you to also begin generating feelings of Unconditional Love.

(Silence)

And sometimes you might have a chant or a mantra that you say to get you into this space like, "Love, Gratitude, Hollow Bone." Or you may have your own mantra that you might say. Or maybe you have a memory of a beautiful experience with a two-legged or four-legged, in which you just felt so much Unconditional Love. Or possibly an experience with Source Energy, a straight direct experience with Source, in whatever way you define Source. Maybe you were out in nature and you just felt at one and at peace with all life everywhere.

(Silence)

So, whatever it is that will help you to embody more Love, just allow yourself to be in that space and to allow all of that Love to begin filling up your heart space, both your energetic and your physical space. Filling up kind of like water fills up a container. As it pours in, it fills from the bottom to the top, and as that Unconditional Love continues to flood in, what happens is that the Unconditional Love floods out of your heart space and begins filling up your physical form. Again, just like a container, from the bottom to the top. So, from the bottoms of your feet, filling up every cell in your body with this Unconditional Love, and hiding no place from this Love.

(Silence)

Really feeling that, and letting it fill up all the way to the top until it overflows into your physical energetic layer of your energy field. Again, filling from the bottom to the top, and hiding no place from this Love. Each layer that gets filled, you just start feeling kind of like some padding is being added to you as this wonderful, loving material is just being wrapped around you like cotton gauze. It's soft, and it's warm, and it's comforting. It's loving.

(Silence)

And then it spills over into your emotional layer, and again you're filling up from the bottom to the top, adding just another layer of this wonderful Unconditional Love wrapping all around you, making you feel so comfortable and at peace and at one, loved and supported.

(Silence)

Spilling over into your mental energetic layer, filling up from the bottom to the top. Knowing that you are loved and supported and healing any belief systems that would be in the way of knowing this.

(Silence)

Filling up until that spills over into your spiritual layer, which also encompasses your light body. This is a very vast layer, and may take a little bit longer to fill up with Unconditional Love because it is so big. But again, hide no place from this Love. When this layer is full, you'll find it a beautiful place to be, and it's perfect to just sit for a moment or two, and just be there. Be this Love. This is the beginning of The Hollow Bone of Healing. There isn't anything you have to do. You are so deeply and profoundly connected in that Unconditional Love that that's all that matters. Just feel that, know that, and be that.

(Silence)

From this place, you may invite in the presence of that who is the highest and best for this session. You may see, sense, or know in some way, or just intend that you are connecting heart-to-heart, feeling that wave of Love that is being sent to you. Really allow yourself to receive this, and take this into every layer. When you're complete, send it back, and know that this Love is being received. It's very important to your helper to feel your Love.

(Silence)

And as your helper takes it in, Love is magnified about ten times before your helper sends it right back to you. Now, allow yourself to open your heart and really receive all this, gratefully, with appreciation, with more Love. And, when you send it back, know it's being received.

(Silence)

One last time, this Love is multiplying to the nth degree and then being sent back to you, and you are feeling this wave of Love between you that is almost beyond human understanding. So, just feel that and be that for a moment.

[Silence]

When you're ready, you can merge entirely with your helper's energy using any of the methods that appeal to you. It's really easy to be together, and during this time you may receive messages, you may receive some healing, or you may just be in that energy. Open all your senses, step into The Hollow Bone of Healing, and just allow whatever is for your highest and best to happen. Seeing, sensing, feeling, knowing whatever is best for you right now.

[Silence]

It is enough by merging with your helper to open the door to miracles. Feeling a sphere of energy around you known as your energy field, feeling, sensing, knowing the boundaries of your energy field, playfully expanding them or relaxing them as you wish. Getting in touch with the sphere of energy in ways that work for you.

(Silence)

Find that sphere of energy, and put your conscious awareness there so you are sensing, feeling and knowing that place in a way that is right for you. And if you did nothing else but this meditation every day for 5 minutes, this is a great meditation of stillness and balance and wholeness all by itself. But today, we're going a little further.

So from this place of stillness and wholeness, your natural state of being, I invite you to go into a memory of something you have longed for all your life. This is a really deep memory so just allow it to surface for you. A dream or a memory that would make you so happy, it's almost too good to be true.

(Silence)

Just allow it to come to the surface, and know that if it's not coming right now, it can come in twenty-four to forty-eight hours. It can come in your daydreams, your night dreams, or something someone says that jars your memory and brings to the surface what you need to know right now.

Maybe something you read, or you're outdoors walking, and it just appears as a thought, but it's a thought you've had before. A beautiful memory of something that would make your life so incredible, so wonderful that this is what the universe wishes for you. That's why you've had this thought, this memory. Just take it into the stillness of your heart space, and nurture it lovingly.

Maybe even do this daily for the next week until you can work with it more. But for now, just suspend all thought of how to do this. Just hold it in a loving embrace because this dream or memory is what would make you so deliriously happy it's almost beyond human understanding. And the universe would love to bring it to you.

(Silence)

Just hold that and hold that and send it Love, feed it with Love. And then, just bring it into that heart space with both hands, anchoring it there in that stillness. No matter what it is, the universe will bring it to you, this or something better. And all the steps you need to make it happen will come in for you in the next few weeks, few months, and in its divine timing.

And when that feels complete for now, your helper will disengage from the merge and you can bring yourself back into your body and back into your room.

Reflections

- I was able to be in Unconditional Love in this way:
- My spirit helper was:
- My sense of my sphere was like this:
- My dreams or memory of what I choose to create looks like this:

Want to know and experience the power of Sacred Geometry Activations plus access Your Sacred Control Panel of Healing and be entrained to Illuminated Reiki™, the universal healing energy that quickly heals the heart of all issues? Check out Take the Training on

HealingAngelProtocol.com for more information or to register for the course. (Levels I and II are prerequisites for Level III, Healing DNA with Sacred Geometry.

Next: Part II: The Self-Healing Techniques

Chapter Four: The Portal of Love and Light

PART II

The Self-Healing Techniques while being The Hollow Bone of Healing

CHAPTER FOUR

The Portal of Love and Light

People don't believe me when I tell them I'm a magician
who makes portals to other worlds. So I tell them
I'm a writer instead.

~Genesis Quihuis

Background: The Portal of Love and Light

This technique actually is not officially in **The Healing Angel Protocol™ Therapy**. It was created primarily for this manual, but we are adding it to the 5-Day Live Immersion Training and to the Advanced Planetary Healing Techniques used by the graduates of **The Healing Angel Protocol™ Therapy.**

One of the things I love about creating portals of Love and Light is how easy the technique is. Once you have mastered The Merge, it is simple to merge with both The Spirit of Love and The Spirit of Light simultaneously, creating a portal of Love and Light. This portal is permanent, filled with Unconditional Love, positively affects all life in that area, and is a gift to the planet. Through intention, multiple portals can be created at the same time, further enriching the healing to the world.

Once again, we spend a lot of time in the energy of Unconditional Love. Feeling it, sensing it, becoming it. When we're completely surrounded and filled with Love, we invite in The Spirit of Love and The Spirit of Light. Beginning with The Spirit of Love, we spend time sharing that loving energy back and forth, allowing it to build and build. When you're ready, merge your field entirely with The Spirit of Love. Seeing, sensing, feeling, knowing that Love. Receiving messages and healing if appropriate, or just having a sense of Peace.

While still merged, you turn your awareness to The Spirit of Light and spend time sharing loving energy back and forth, allowing it to build and build. When you're ready, merge your field entirely with The Spirit of Light. Seeing, sensing, feeling, knowing that Love. Receiving messages and healing if appropriate, or just having a sense of Peace. Feeling the difference between the two Spirits as their energies are very distinctive.

To create the portal, simply hold the intention for any and all places in the world you'd like to offer Love and Light. Possibly your front door where people enter your home, your meditation room, or your healing room. Perhaps your office, school, car, or your computer. Or your machines. Or a place that has been devastated by a tornado, hurricane, or earthquake. There are no limits. Intention is all it takes to create a portal anywhere in the world.

When your intentions have been set, imagine yourself holding hands with The Spirit of Love and The Spirit of Light. Holding the Love. Being the Love. Stating your intentions for portals. It's really that easy. You simply hold that energy for as long as you like, and it is so. Portals are created. You'll know it because they are palpable. People feel them, sense them, and react differently, from a higher state of consciousness than before.

When The Spirit of Love and The Spirit of Light first gave me this technique, I performed it at my desk in my office. I intended that the portals be my desk, computer, office, meditation room, front door and myself. I chose to be a walking, talking portal of Love and Light.

As I began, the first thing that happened was I felt such overwhelming Love! It was much stronger than I had previously encountered with any of the other techniques. I was so overwhelmed with Love, I had chills, goosebumps, and tears. My heart overflowed. I sat in profound silence for several minutes.

After I merged with The Spirit of Love and The Spirit of Light, I sat in complete silence, feeling such intense Love, feeling the portals as they were created, and knowing that something profound was happening, even if I wasn't sure what it was. Throughout the day I received confirmation about the portals as my day proceeded effortlessly, easily, and tirelessly. Everyone I spoke to was pleasant, kind, and helpful. Additional intentions were instantly manifested. I felt no stress or worry in spite of the fact I was behind on a few major projects. Everything just flowed.

Upon sharing this with some of the graduates of **The Healing Angel Protocol™ Therapy**, they had similar reactions. Feeling the gratitude of the earth for this gift. Noticing the changes in peoples' energies as they entered the portals. Experiencing the effortlessness of daily living around the portal. Feeling the profound effects of instant manifestation.

And it all begins with Love.

Access your Free Guided Meditation: The Portal of Love and Light here: https://phoenix-rising-star.mykajabi.com/ offers/E8xyELD2

Meditation: The Portal of Love and Light

Welcome to The Portal of Love and Light. This is a beautiful technique for clearing any toxicity energetically from your place or a place in nature and enriching the energy of your space, or a place that honors free will and chooses to receive this. We're working with The Spirit of Love and The Spirit of Light to create this.

So to begin, I invite you to think about all the places where you'd like to create Portals of Love and Light. Not only are they clearing tools, they bring in that element of Unconditional Love to all life that passes through them, and they're permanent. You can create them with this technique anywhere in the world, again honoring free will.

So I invite you think about all the places where you'd like a Portal of Love and Light. Beginning with the place where you live. Maybe your car, your office, your meditation room, your computer. Maybe you. Maybe you'd like to be a walking, talking Portal of Love and Light. This is also something you can do when you're out in nature, and you'd just like to give back to nature for all the Love you're feeling there, and all the connection you have to all life everywhere.

So take a moment to think about all the perfect places where you'd like to have a Portal of Love and Light.

(Silence)

When you're ready, I invite you to begin filling yourself with Unconditional Love to the best of your ability, really feeling, sensing, and knowing it. Maybe through an experience you've had, or a memory, or through key words or phrases that work for you. Just begin opening your heart to Unconditional Love and allowing it to flow through you, hiding no place from this Love.

As this Love is expanding into your entire field, take your time to appreciate it and allow yourself to feel that cocoon of Love that is wrapping itself around you.

(Silence)

When you feel really complete with that Love, invite in The Spirit of Love and The Spirit of Light to be with you.

Invite them into the tiny space of your heart, that energetic space that's behind your literal heart. Finding a place where you can be comfortable together, either sitting or standing or in some position that is comfortable for you. Feeling the Love that is emanating from both of them to you. We'll begin with The Spirit of Love first. With your senses, just become aware of how The Spirit of Love appears to you. Maybe seeing, sensing or feeling, hearing particular tones or frequencies, or the smell of flowers. However you perceive The Spirit of Love.

And above all, as you open your heart, feel that wave of Love that is coming to you from The Spirit of Love. Feel it as it fills your physical form and your energetic form. Taking that in, and taking that in.

When you're ready, you can give this back to The Spirit of Love. Know that The Spirit of Love is taking it in and is so grateful for what you've sent. The Spirit of Love is taking it in and amplifying it before sending it back to you again. This time when you feel it, it's even more powerful, and it's going to those tiny hidden places that even you've forgotten about. Just allow yourself to be filled with this Love. When you're ready, just send it back to the Spirit of Love, where it's being received, and amplified and one last time being given back to you. Washing over you, completely filling you with this Unconditional Love. It's at this point you can merge your frequency entirely with this beautiful being. As you do that, you may receive messages or healing or you may just have this wonderful, comfortable feeling of peace.

(Silence)

When that's complete for now, just stay merged with The Spirit of Love as you turn your conscious awareness to The Spirit of Light. Open your heart and feel the Love that is coming to you from the Spirit of Light. Discerning that it feels slightly different from The Spirit of Love. But it's still pure Love. Taking it in and allowing it to move through you wherever you need it the most. Then, when you're ready, just send it right back to The Spirit of Light, knowing that it's being gratefully received and amplified. Coming right back to you in that expansive state, and it moves all the way through you, even into those tiny places you forgot about. Really feeling that and taking it in, and sending it back when you're ready, knowing that it's gratefully received and expanded. One last time it's being sent right back to you where it's going everywhere throughout your physical being and your energy field, hiding no place from this Love. At this point you can merge entirely with The Spirit of Light. You may receive messages or healing or simply have a wonderful feeling of peace.

(Silence)

Be aware that you are now in a place of holding hands with The Spirit of Love and The Spirit of Light, one is on your right and one is on your left. Together you are forming a circle. It is this circle that becomes a Portal. A Portal of Light and Love that clears and heals and brings more Love and is permanent. As you are a part of this Portal, I invite you to think of your list of intended places for this Portal. With every place you intend, that Portal will automatically be created there, honoring the free will of whoever has that space. And every time you think of a new place, feel the Love amplifying within you. That Love from The Spirit of Love, The Spirit of Light and the Portal you are now creating in each and every place.

(Silence)

You'll know when it's complete for now because the energy will subtly shift. You'll still feel that powerful connection to The Spirit of Love and The Spirit of Light, but it's just subtly different because it feels complete now. So for now, just stay in your Portal space. Really feeling this. Noting the clearing and the cleansing, and the Love that replaces that. Really knowing you are making a huge difference in the world, with every Portal you are intending. For this we give thanks. And so it is.

Reflection

- I chose to place Portals in these places:
- What I sensed about each Portal:
- My reactions while creating the Portals:
- My reactions after creating the Portals:
- Other places I can also create Portals:

Would you like to attend the 5-Day Live Immersion and do this with a group? Imagine the difference we can make in the world! Check out Take the Training on HealingAngel-Protocol.com for more information or to register.

Next: Part III: How to Live *The Hollow Bone of Healing*.

Part III

How to Live
The Hollow Bone of Healing

CHAPTER ONE

Meditation—all by itself—may offer more to the health of
a modern American than all the pharmaceutical
remedies put together.

~ **Dawson Church,** *The Genie in Your Genes: Epigen-
etic Medicine and the New Biology of Intention*

As I have stated, this work is not just a modality we turn to
when we're hurting. It is a way of living. I use meditation
daily as my tool of choice for connecting to the Quantum
Field of Source Energy. I teach **The Healing Angel Protocol**™
with guided meditations. I merge frequently, if not daily, for any
reason: to feel better about myself, to receive the highest advice for
inspired action, for healing, for messages, for miracles. For more
information and scientific research on guided meditation, visit our
website: https://www.HealingAngelProtocol.com

I, Phoenix Rising Star, continue to surround myself with the loving community of The Hollow Bone Society members who understand me, and for whom I don't have to explain myself. And they
connect because that is what they are looking for as well. I continue
to offer personal and planetary healing because that's in alignment
with my soul purpose. I offer the planetary healings free of charge
and open to the public because that's how I'm guided.

Some of my students share how they live *The Hollow Bone of
Healing*.

Janel: " Since learning The Healing Angel Protocol™, I have felt such a loving change in my life. I can stop my ego when it starts to run amok. I can forgive myself when it does and reconnect with the divine that never left me. One of the most profound things you shared with our class was the question, 'How would Love answer that question?' The Angel Merge is living in that state of Love bliss."

Grace: "The HAP™ is a stand alone healing modality. However, we can take it so much further. I allow my emotions to get the best of me sometimes and act like a runaway train. When I feel my emotions begin to build, I immediately step into the energy of The HAP™. I drop back into my heart and feel the Unconditional Love and ask for an angel to come and merge. When I feel clear, I ask for clarity of the situation and how to best move forward. Now, this all happens in less than 3 minutes. It has become a vital tool in coping with daily stress with a lot more ease and grace than I've ever had!"

Priestess Eylah: "By learning to merge with the angels, you unify with ALL life and understand its true purpose!"

Flo: "By merging with the Angels you learn to Love and Trust yourself more each and every day. They help you to see the beauty that is you while you get healing for this and other lifetimes with ease and grace."

Patricia: "I am in constant contact seeing each step which keeps me secure, calm and in tune effortlessly. My life is as effortless as breathing and merging with my Angels. I trust without trying. I hear my Angels without effort. I feel connected so I feel deep, fulfilling peace and community even when I am alone. I am magnetically attracting soul family and abundance each day. I know who I am and my purpose and it is evident in form. Each day is truly fulfilling but easy. I no longer have basic emotions....fear,

    scarcity, anger, jealousy..... I am truly loving and enjoying
    my life even through challenges that stretch me!"

As for me, I trust. I act on my guidance. My life is amazing and filled
with constant miracles.

This is all available to you.

It is my belief that these processes will open the doors to a life that
is amazing and filled with miracles.

And if you wish to go farther than where this self-healing takes you,
there are ways to do that too.

When you want or need more, visit **www.HealingAngelProtocol.
com** and check out the pages **Find a Practitioner** or **Take the
Training**. Just having a session with a trained professional will jump-
start your healing and manifestations. Or for deeper transformation,
purchase the **Home Study Course** with the **5-Day Immersion
Training**. In this way, you'll have your community of like-minded,
like-hearted individuals who totally understand you, and you'll have
support as you move through merging into your beautiful and miraculous state. Creating the change you wish, not the change you don't.

For free information and healing videos and to be a part of our community, join our Hollow Bone Society here: **https://phoenix-
rising-star.mykajabi.com/offers/FEdBeBWm**

This society is one of community sharing and learning, plus you'll
receive updates on new trainings and information before the public does.

And if you like this book, please consider leaving a customer review
on Amazon.

You will help empower a lot of people on their path of self-healing!

Thank you for reading this and changing your world.

Phoenix Rising Star

Printed in Great Britain
by Amazon

10835740R00050